About the Book

What are teeth made of? How do teeth grow? What different kinds of teeth are there? How can you help your teeth be strong and healthy?

Winifred Hammond answers all these questions, and many more, in this fascinating book. Find out precisely how and when teeth are formed. See the different kinds of teeth, and learn their names and functions. Discover the causes of dental diseases and how best to prevent them.

Mrs. Hammond directs her book to boys and girls in the early grades. She uses a simple and direct approach which is also carefully researched and comprehensive. She presents facts about teeth which are observed and verified by the child himself through easy projects. As the child makes his own observations, facts suddenly become new and meaningful.

Photographs, drawings, and diagrams, illustrate the text. A welcome introduction to the study of teeth, this book can be used by children on their own, in groups, or with a dentist or teacher.

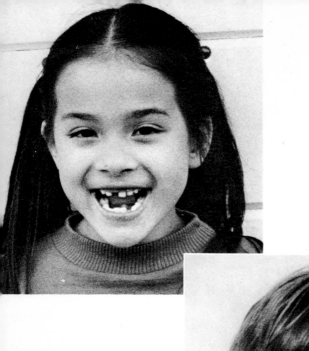

Dental Adviser
Gilbert V. Oliver, D.M.D., F.I.C.D.
School of Dentistry
University of California, San Francisco

The Riddle of Teeth

by

Winifred G. Hammond

With best wishes to Meredith and all the Youngs

Winifred G. Hammond.

Coward, McCann & Geoghegan
New York

To Megan

Photo Credits

Bureau of Sport Fisheries & Wildlife, 19 (left, top and bottom). Department of Bacteriology, University of California, Berkeley, 33. Chester Fong, DDS, 23. Winifred Hammond, 8, 11, 12, 13, 19 (right, top and center), 29, 37, 43, 52 (courtesy Frank Kami, DDS). Hammond and Poulton, 28, 30 (bottom, left and right). National Institutes of Health, 32, 34, 35, 56 and 57. W. Paden, DDS, 27. Donald R. Poulton, DDS, 27, 30 (top, left and right). School of Dentistry, University of California, San Francisco, 12, 24 (left and right), 26, 31, 41, 49, 50, 59. Smithsonian Institution, 16 (left and right), 17.

CONTENTS

RIDDLES

1. Why are teeth like trains?
2. What tooth is like a letter plus a number?
3. Which are the smartest teeth?
4. What animal has teeth but never chews?
5. What animal uses his teeth to pull himself?
6. What two letters make us lose our teeth?
7. What animal may have two holes in its teeth but no decay?
8. Why is a tooth like a king?

If you want to know the answers to these riddles you will find them in this book.

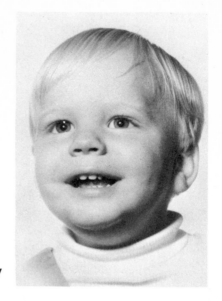

Three-year-old-boy has all his primary teeth.

PRIMARY TEETH

You know that very young babies don't have any teeth that we can see.

Ask your mother if she remembers when your first tooth appeared. Were you six or seven months old?

Do you have any baby pictures that show your teeth?

When you were eight months old, you probably had eight teeth — four upper and four lower.

When you were three years old, you must have had twenty teeth. This is a full set of baby or primary teeth.

Teeth are like trains and airplanes. They usually come in according to a timetable.

A few babies have teeth a little earlier or later than the timetable says they will. Once in a while a baby has a few teeth when it is born.

Here is a tooth timetable. Dental scientists studied thousands of children to get the numbers in the timetable.

THE PRIMARY TEETH

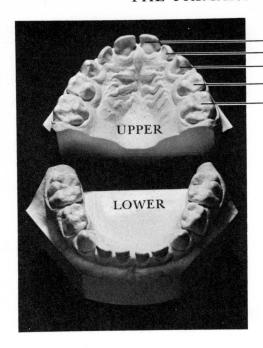

CENTRAL INCISOR
LATERAL INCISOR
CUSPID (CANINE)
FIRST MOLAR
SECOND MOLAR

UPPER

LOWER

LOWER BABY TEETH	AGE AT WHICH TEETH APPEAR
Central incisors (in-SIGH-zers)	6 months
Lateral incisors	7½ months
Cuspids (KUS-pids)	16 months
First molars (MO-lers)	12 months
Second molars	20 months

UPPER BABY TEETH	
Central incisors	7 months
Lateral incisors	9 months
Cuspids	18 months
First molars	14 months
Second molars	24 months

[Riddle (1) — Teeth come in according to a timetable.]

NEW TEETH FOR OLD

Each year you grew bigger. Your head grew and your jaws grew. But your teeth didn't grow. Try to imagine how your baby teeth would look in an adult mouth.

Fortunately, when you were about six years old, a second timetable took over. You were starting to get a whole new set of teeth. Some of your second or permanent teeth began to grow through your gums.

The first permanent teeth to grow through the gums were molars or chewing teeth. They came in back of your

TEETH AT ABOUT SIX YEARS OF AGE

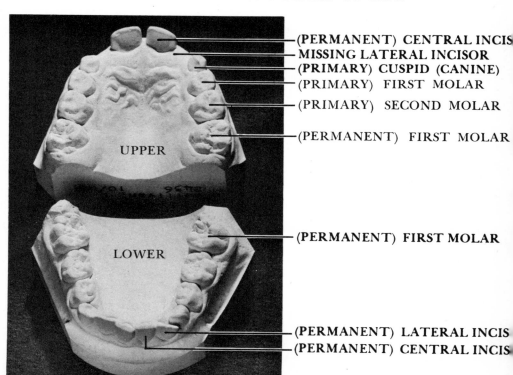

— (PERMANENT) CENTRAL INCIS
— MISSING LATERAL INCISOR
— (PRIMARY) CUSPID (CANINE)
— (PRIMARY) FIRST MOLAR
— (PRIMARY) SECOND MOLAR
— (PERMANENT) FIRST MOLAR

UPPER

LOWER

— (PERMANENT) FIRST MOLAR

— (PERMANENT) LATERAL INCIS
— (PERMANENT) CENTRAL INCIS

Seven-year-old girl is
missing her front teeth.

primary (baby) teeth. There was room for them because
your jaws grew after your primary teeth were in place.

Two of these new molars came in your upper jaw, one
on the left side and one on the right. Two came in the
lower jaw. These four teeth are called the six-year molars.
The molars crush and grind food.

About this time one of your lower front teeth became
loose. Did you pull it out yourself?

This front tooth was loose because its roots were gone.
The roots were absorbed or dissolved because a new tooth
was growing under it.

DIFFERENT KINDS OF TEETH

Count your teeth. Put a finger between your cheek and your teeth. Start counting at the back tooth and move forward and around.

Feel the shape of each tooth. Notice that they come in pairs, one left and one right. What is the shape of your front teeth? These are the incisors. This means cutters. The two front teeth are central (center) incisors. On each side of them is a lateral (side) incisor.

Find your four cuspid teeth. Feel their pointed tips or cusps. Another name for these teeth is canine (KAY-nine) or doglike. Look at the picture of a dog. How do his canines, or cuspids, differ from yours?

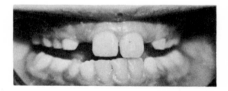

Permanent incisors have replaced primary incisors.

Dog shows his long canine teeth.

Back of the canines are teeth with two sharp ridges or cusps, the bicuspids (BY-kus-pids), or two cusps.

[Riddle (2) — The canine (K-9) tooth.]

WISDOM TEETH

By the time you are fifteen years old you should have all your permanent teeth except the third molars. These are called wisdom teeth.

Wisdom teeth appear between the ages of sixteen and thirty, or even later. Sometimes there is no room for them in the jaws, and they grow under the roots of the other teeth. This makes trouble which can be corrected only by a dentist. Not everybody has four wisdom teeth. A few people don't have any.

[Riddle (3) — The wisdom teeth are the smartest]

13

THE PERMANENT TEETH

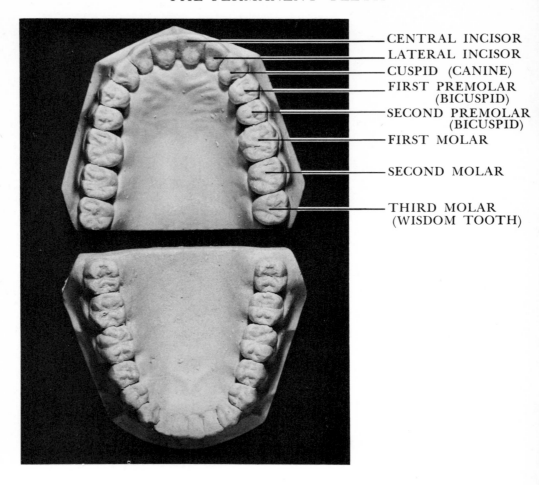

CENTRAL INCISOR
LATERAL INCISOR
CUSPID (CANINE)
FIRST PREMOLAR (BICUSPID)
SECOND PREMOLAR (BICUSPID)
FIRST MOLAR
SECOND MOLAR
THIRD MOLAR (WISDOM TOOTH)

TIMETABLE FOR PERMANENT TEETH TO GROW THROUGH GUMS

	AGE (years) Upper Teeth	AGE (years) Lower Teeth
Central incisors	7– 8	6– 7
Lateral incisors	8– 9	7– 8
Cuspids	11–12	9–10
First bicuspids	10–11	10–12
Second bicuspids	10–12	11–12
First molars	6– 7	6– 7
Second molars	12–13	11–13
Third molars or wisdom teeth	17–21	17–21

PROJECT

PROJECT — TO MAKE A STOP-AND-GO PICTURE OF YOUR TEETH

WHAT YOU NEED

1 large mirror
1 flashlight
paper, pencil, red crayon, green crayon

WHAT YOU DO

Stand in front of the mirror. Shine the flashlight into your
  mouth. Examine your teeth.

List your primary teeth. Be careful that you don't mis-
  take the first permanent molars (six-year molars) for
  baby teeth. They fool lots of people.

List your permanent teeth.

With the help of the pictures on pages 9 and 14 draw a
  picture of your upper and your lower jaw. Draw in
  your teeth. Color the primary ones green, because
  they will *go*. Color the permanent teeth red because
  they will *stop* and stay with you.

Get your friends to make pictures of their teeth.

Now compare pictures.

FOSSIL TEETH

Many boys and girls collect fossils. These are the remains or traces of remains of plants or animals that lived long ago.

There are many kinds of fossils. Tracks of animals left in soft mud that later hardened to stone are called fossils.

Petrified fossils are plant or animal tissues that were partly or entirely replaced by minerals. The Petrified Forest in Arizona is full of trunks of trees that lived 160,000,000 years ago. The wood was gradually replaced by bright-colored agate.

Teeth are among the commonest fossils because they are the hardest parts of animals and don't rot easily. Fossil teeth may or may not be petrified.

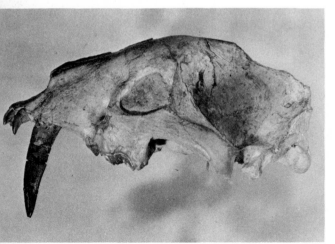

Saber-toothed tiger fossil

Lower jaw fossil of fish-eating giant lizard

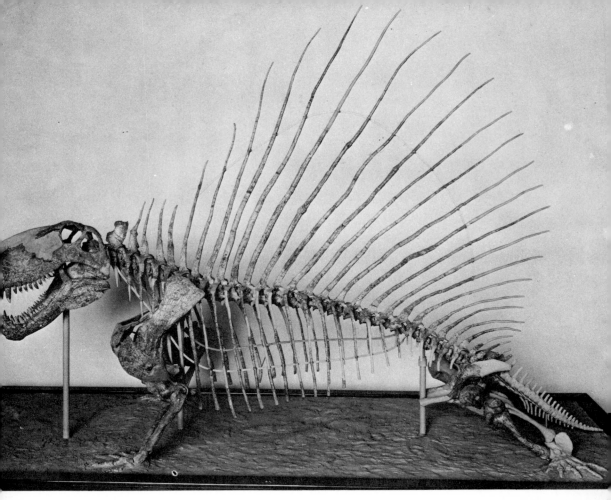

Fossil skeleton of flesh-eat-
ing sail lizard

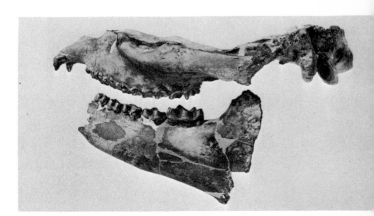

Fossil jawbone of leaf-eat-
ing mammal

17

USES OF TEETH

Animals use their teeth in many ways besides chewing and biting. The meat eaters use their teeth to defend themselves and to kill other animals for food.

Beavers and porcupines gnaw trees with their incisors. A beaver can cut through a four-inch-thick aspen tree in less than fifteen minutes.

Gophers use their incisors to dig holes for their burrows (homes) under the ground.

Vampire bats use their razor-sharp incisors to scrape small grooves through the skin of sleeping animals and birds so that they can lap up the blood that seeps out. Their victims don't wake up. A scientist said he had been bitten many times when he was handling these bats. He didn't even know he had been bitten until he saw the bloody places on his skin.

Snakes have teeth but do not chew their food. They use their teeth to catch and hold their prey; then they swallow it whole. The rattlesnake has holes in two big teeth called fangs. The snake injects poison into its victims through these holes.

[Riddle (4) — Snakes swallow their food without chewing
it.]
[Riddle (7) — Some snakes have fangs with holes down the
middle. These are cavities but not decay.]

Shark gets new teeth whenever he loses some.

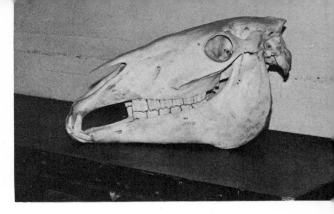

Horse skull shows teeth for biting and chewing grass.

Porcupine gnaws the bark of a tree.

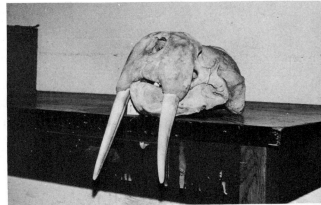

Walrus has long canines and no incisors.

Ocelot shows his lower canines.

PROJECT

PROJECT — TO MAKE A POSTER TO ILLUSTRATE DIFFERENT KINDS OF ANIMAL TEETH AND THE MANY WAYS ANIMALS USE THEIR TEETH

Here are some other animals that use their teeth for things besides chewing:

Walrus — Uses his long canines (tusks) to dig for mussels and clams. Also, he uses them to pull his heavy body from the water onto the ice.

Elephant — Uses his teeth like levers (tools) to pull down trees and lift logs.

Horse — Uses his front teeth (incisors) like scissors to snip off grass.

Wolf and wild dog — Use their canines to catch and hold their prey.

Rats and mice — Use their sharp incisors to gnaw bark, nuts, and hard-coated seeds. In houses and barns they may gnaw holes through wood to get into places where food is stored.

[Riddle (5) — The walrus sometimes pulls himself with his teeth.]

WHAT IS A TOOTH?

What is a tooth? Let's look at one.

Ask your dentist to save a permanent tooth for you which he has pulled. If you can't get a real tooth, use the picture on this page.

About one-third of the tooth, the crown, showed beyond the gum line. The roots were in holes (sockets) in the jawbone. The holes formed gradually as the tooth developed.

A hard shiny material covers the crown. This is enamel (ee-NA-mel).

[Riddle (8) — A tooth and a king both have crowns.]

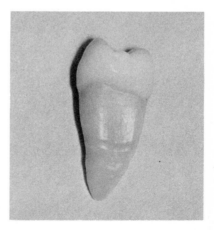

A tooth

CROSS SECTION OF A TOOTH.

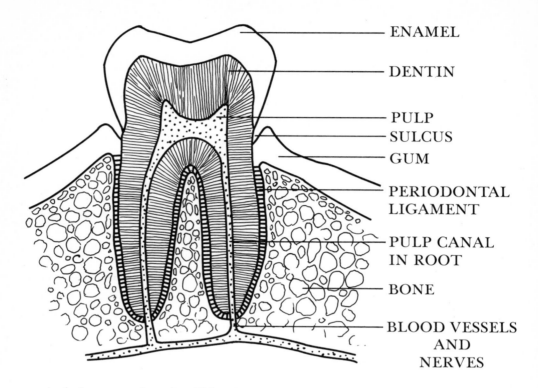

- ENAMEL
- DENTIN
- PULP
- SULCUS
- GUM
- PERIODONTAL LIGAMENT
- PULP CANAL IN ROOT
- BONE
- BLOOD VESSELS AND NERVES

Ask your dentist if he can get a permanent tooth sawed in half vertically (from top to bottom) at a dental laboratory. Or look at the diagram on this page.

Now you can see that the enamel is not very thick. Under it is the dentin (DEN-tin). Dentin is much the same as the material our bones are made of. It is hard, but not as hard as enamel.

The small canal in the center of the tooth has branches that go into the roots. This was filled with pulp made of nerves, blood vessels, and other soft tissues. The nerves and blood vessels joined others in the jaw. These tissues were torn when the tooth was removed.

TEETH UNDER A MICROSCOPE

With a microscope you can see that both the enamel and the dentin are made of tiny rods. The rods have six sides like the cells of a honeycomb. A tooth contains millions of them.

Each rod grows from a single cell. At first it is like a little empty tube. Soon it begins to fill with chemicals from the blood. These chemicals are mainly calcium (KAL-si-um) and phosphorus (FOS-for-us), also found in bones. They gradually calcify (KAL-si-fy) and change to a harder material. The hardened tubes (rods) are held together by a softer cement.

Dentin is as hard as bone. Enamel is even harder. It is the hardest of all tissues in the body.

Microscopic section of a growing tooth (1) dentin (2) periodontal ligament (3) jawbone (4) enamel

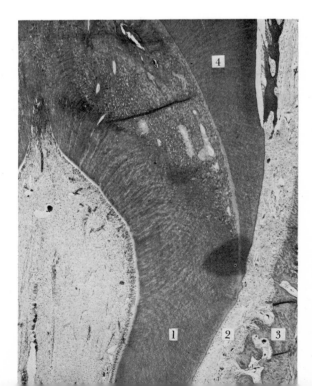

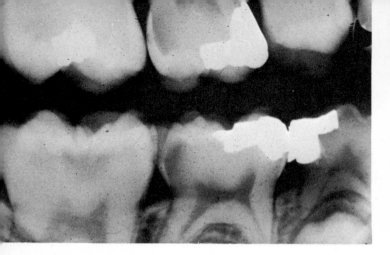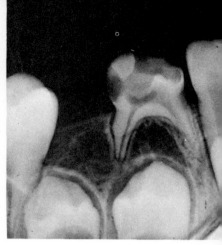

X rays of teeth. Right: A permanent tooth grows beneath the gum.

X-RAY PICTURES

Another way to examine teeth is by X rays. These rays come from a special kind of electric bulb called an X-ray tube. They are not like ordinary light rays. They can go right through your body. They don't go through the bones as easily as through the flesh, so the bones cast shadows.

We can't see X rays or the shadows they make, with our eyes. We can see the light and dark places they make on photographic film.

When X-ray pictures are made of the mouth, the gums let more X rays through than the teeth do. Fillings in cavities show clearly because the tooth lets more X rays go through than the metal of the fillings.

The dentist can find cavities that are under the enamel or under the gums, by making and looking at X-ray pictures. He can tell whether or not the roots are healthy and in the right positions.

WHAT HOLDS TEETH IN THE JAWS?

Teeth are held in holes or sockets in the jawbones. They are held tight in these sockets by bundles of tough little strings or fibers (FY-bers).

The dentist calls these strings the periodontal (per-i-oh-DONT-al) ligament. Periodontal means *all around the teeth*. The periodontal ligament is torn loose when a tooth is pulled.

The ligament allows a tooth to move slightly in the jaw. It acts something like a shock absorber in an automobile. It protects the tooth from the shocks of biting and chewing.

Hold one of your permanent teeth with your thumb and finger. Try to rock it from side to side. You probably can feel it move slightly.

Microscopic section of a tooth, enlarged (1) dentin (2) periodontal ligament (3) jawbone

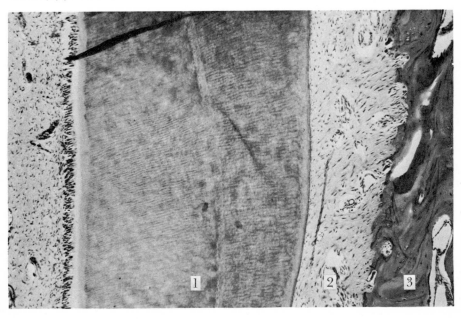

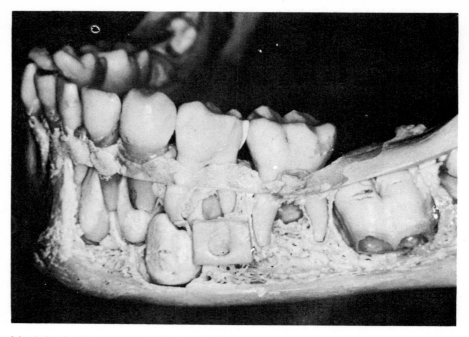

Model of a five-year-old's teeth. See the permanent teeth growing beneath the primary teeth.

TOOTH BUDS

How long do you think it takes to grow a tooth? Would you say a few days, a month, a year, or longer? You would be right if you guessed either of the last two answers.

Under a powerful microscope a beginning tooth looks like a tiny flower bud.

The day you were born, an X-ray picture of your mouth would have shown all your baby teeth in your jaws in different stages of growth.

Also, the X ray would have shown the tooth buds of some of your adult teeth.

A GOOD BITE

By the time you were three years old you had twenty baby teeth fully grown. Probably these teeth were well spaced and fitted together to give you a good bite and a good chewing surface, called the occlusion (ah-KLOO-shun).

Often this good occlusion, which most young children have, changes as the permanent teeth come in.

Your new teeth are larger than your baby teeth. Did these larger teeth seem to crowd one another when they came through the gums? Maybe your upper incisors were pushed outward to give you "buck teeth." Or some teeth may have turned sideways.

Another cause of poor occlusion of permanent teeth is the early loss of a baby tooth. Did you lose one of your baby teeth long before a new one was ready to take its place?

X ray of head showing buckteeth

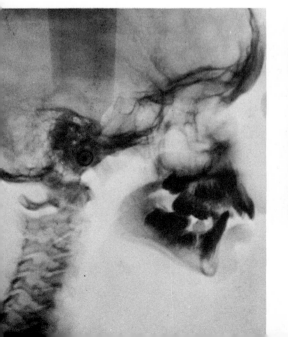

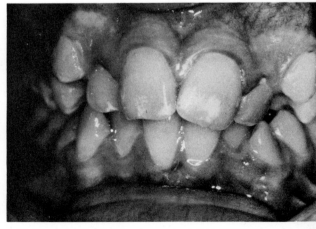

Crowded teeth

MOVING TEETH

You probably went to see your dentist when your permanent teeth began to come in. If they were coming in crowded or out of position, your dentist said, "You'd better see an orthodontist [or-tho-DON-tist]. He specializes in correcting this kind of tooth trouble."

Do you remember what the orthodontist did?

First he photographed your face and head. Then he took an X-ray picture of your head, like the one on page 27. Next he made a plaster of Paris model of your teeth and jaws. (See below.)

a. Soft impression material put in trays

b. Trays fitted in mouth

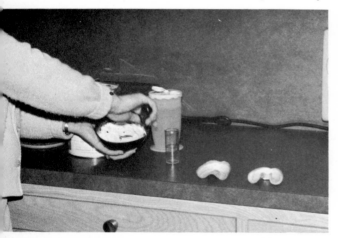
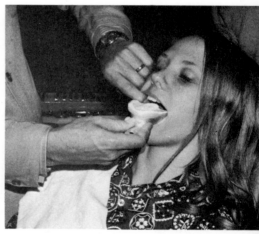

c. Firm impression made

d. Plaster of paris makes cast of impress

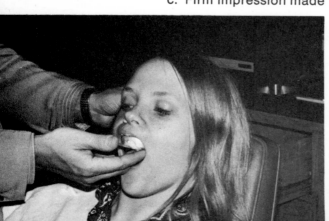

Boy wearing an elastic neckband

He told you, "After I study all these, I'll know what needs to be done."

Perhaps the orthodontist said that moving a tooth is like moving a post in the ground. The post will move if you change the shape or position of the hole. A tooth moves when the bony socket (hole) changes.

The bone around a tooth is living. It changes when pressure is put on the tooth. There is no harm either to the bone or to the tooth if it is moved slowly by gentle pressure.

The orthodontist put pressure on your teeth by means of rubber bands and springy wires. He hooked these to metal bands, which he fitted on your teeth. Probably he also gave you an elastic neckband to wear at night. You hooked this to the band on your teeth. This was another way of putting pressure on the teeth that needed to be moved.

Perhaps your mother has small jaws and teeth and your father has big jaws and big teeth. You may have small jaws like your mother's and big teeth like your father's, so your permanent teeth are crowded. The orthodontist decided to remove a few teeth to make room in your jaws for the others. Probably he took out four bicuspids, two upper and two lower.

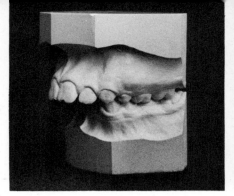

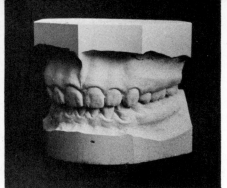

Cast before treatment   Cast after treatment

After two or three years of treatment you hardly knew yourself when you looked in the mirror. Your teeth were evenly spaced in two beautiful curved rows. There was no gap where the bicuspids were removed. You had a good bite.

Did you say, "Well, I sure look a lot better?"

Do you know a child who needs to have his teeth straightened, but his parents can't afford the cost? Tell him to talk to the school nurse or a nurse at a health clinic. Often there is money which can be used for dental care.

It is better to have orthodontic treatment as soon as possible since teeth move more easily in young people. However, orthodontists can straighten teeth of adults in their twenties, thirties, or even forties.

Boy with buckteeth   Boy after treatment

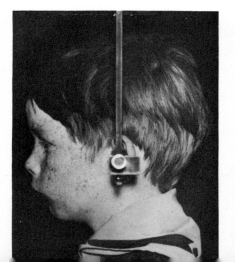

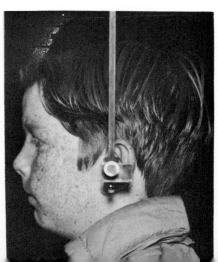

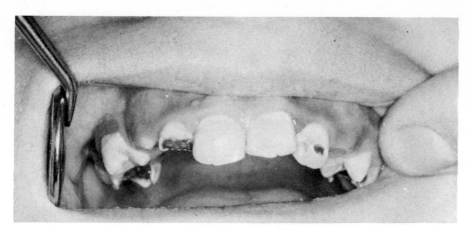

Teeth showing decay

ANCIENT DENTAL DISEASES

Have you ever had a cavity or a toothache? These are caused by a disease, *dental caries* (CARE-ees). In everyday words this is tooth decay.

Another disease which affects the bone and other tissues around the teeth is called *periodontal disease.* The common name for this is pyorrhea (pie-oh-REE-a). Pyorrhea often results in loss of teeth.

Scientists who have examined ancient skulls all over the world say that these diseases have bothered mankind for a very long time.

One Stone Age man who lived in South Africa 100,000 years ago must have had many toothaches. When his skull was found, only thirteen teeth remained. These teeth had fifteen cavities.

[Riddle (6) — Decay (D-K) makes us lose our teeth.]

Hamster used in tooth decay experiments

ANIMALS AND DENTAL DISEASE

Animals, too, have dental disease. Wild apes in the forest have tooth troubles. So do dogs and cats.

If you have a pet that is old, examine his mouth. Do the gums look red or swollen? Perhaps your pet ate hard chunky food when he was young. Now he will eat only soft foods. Often this is a sign that it hurts him to chew.

Other pets, such as white rats and hamsters, get dental caries.

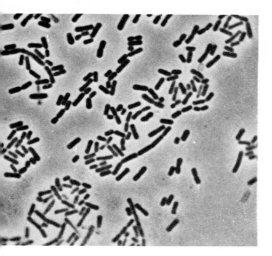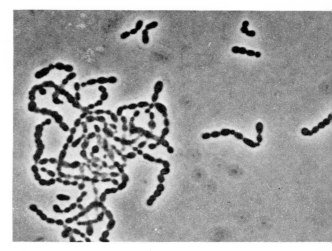

Two kinds of bacteria found in the mouth

BACTERIA IN THE MOUTH

People always have wondered why anything as hard as teeth get cavities so easily. Dental scientists have found some of the reasons.

Everyone has bacteria in his mouth. These are very small one-celled plants. When we look at bacteria with a microscope, we can see three different shapes: round, rod-shaped, and spiral. Some bacteria are harmful to people, but many are not. Often we call the harmful ones germs.

All surfaces of our teeth are covered with a thin film, the bacterial plaque (plak). It is a living glue that sticks so tightly we can't rinse it off with water. Plaque is almost colorless. Besides bacteria, it contains substances from food and the saliva.

If the plaque isn't removed, it becomes thicker, more slimy, and filled with more and more bacteria. Cavities *always begin under plaque.*

33

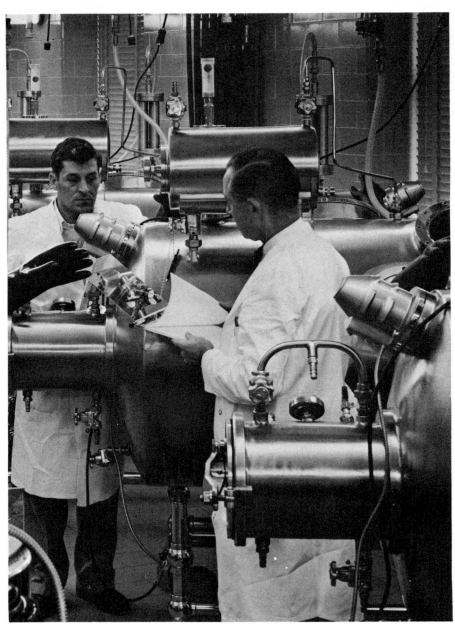

Hamsters are born and live in these germ-free tanks.

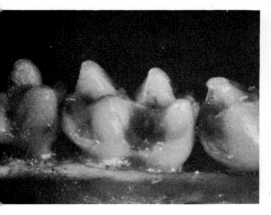

Decay-free hamster teeth   Decayed hamster teeth

DENTAL CARIES EXPERIMENTS

Dental researchers wondered if bacteria could be causing tooth decay. They tried raising rats in germproof cages. Their teeth didn't have even one cavity.

Then bacterial plaque from rats with caries was smeared on the teeth of the rats in the germproof cages. What do you think happened? You're right. The rats without cavities soon had cavities.

One researcher put no-caries animals into cages with others that had caries. Soon all his animals had caries. The no-caries ones had "caught" caries the same way they might catch other diseases.

35

MOUTH BACTERIA MAKE ACID

How do bacteria cause cavities?

Some kinds of bacteria commonly found in the plaque can make a weak acid when certain foods are in the mouth. This is lactic (LAK-tik) acid. Lactic acid is also in sour milk.

The saliva in the mouth can neutralize some of this acid and make it harmless to teeth. But it can't do it on the tooth surface under bacterial plaque.

Here is the way tooth decay is caused:

SOME KINDS OF BACTERIA + FOOD = ACID

ACID + BACTERIAL PLAQUE + TOOTH = DECAY

36

FOODS IN THE MOUTH

You know that you need a good diet so that you will grow a sound body and well-formed teeth. However, good food alone does not prevent decay.

Foods can be divided into three groups. They are proteins (PRO-te-ins), fats, and carbohydrates (car-bo-HIGH-drates). The carbohydrates are either starchy or sugary.

Lean meat, cheese, milk, and eggs are mainly protein foods. Butter, margarine, and meat fat are fatty foods. Bread, crackers, and potatoes are starchy foods. Candy and sweet desserts are sugary foods.

Not all these foods form acid in the mouth at the same rate. For example, raw vegetables form acids very slowly. Carbohydrate foods, especially the sugary ones, form acids rapidly.

Starchy carbohydrates

Sweet carbohydrates

HOW DO WE PREVENT CAVITIES?

Dental researchers say that two of the ways to fight tooth decay are:

1. Reduce the number of acid-forming bacteria by reducing bacterial plaque.
2. Eat less of the foods that form acids easily and quickly.

There is much proof that these methods really do help prevent decay. During World War II sweets were scarce in war-torn countries. After the war dentists examined children in Norway and in Japan. They found that the children had less than one-third the number of cavities that their older brothers and sisters had before the war when sweets were plentiful.

In our own country many young people have stopped rapid decay in their teeth by eating fewer sweets and keeping their teeth clean (reducing plaque).

Also, thousands of diabetic children, who are not allowed sweets, have fewer cavities than their friends who are not diabetic.

HOW MANY SNACKS?

The number of times a day you eat sweets is even more important than the amount of sweets you eat.

Let's say you eat some sugar or a sweet dessert with each of your meals. Then you have a candy bar or some cookies as a snack in the afternoon when you get home from school. Before dinner you are thirsty and you drink a cola. Five times in that one day acid attacked your teeth.

The graph (graf) on this page shows what happened to

SNACKS AND CAVITIES

A Study in West Tennessee, 1956

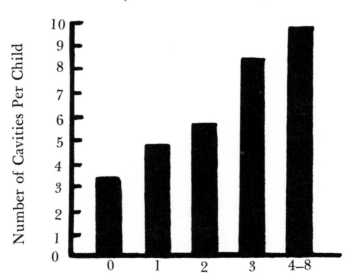

Number of Between-Meal Snacks

700 children, ages five to six years old, in Tennessee when they ate sweet snacks. The lengths of the lines are equal to the number of cavities.

The first line shows what happened to the children who ate sweets only with meals. They had about 3 cavities each. The next line shows the number of cavities of the children who also ate sweets once between meals. "Read" the graph to see how many cavities the children had when they ate four or more sweet snacks between meals.

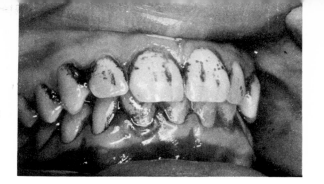

Disclosing tablet stains
plaque.

PROJECT

PROJECT — TO FIND OUT HOW MUCH BACTERIAL PLAQUE IS ON YOUR OWN TEETH

WHAT YOU NEED

Disclosing tablets. You may be able to get a few of these pink tablets from your school nurse or the drugstore. If not, your dentist can order them for you. They are harmless.

WHAT YOU DO

Put one of the tablets in your mouth and chew it well. Do not swallow. When the tablet is all dissolved, your mouth will be full of pink saliva. Rinse this around in your mouth so that it gets to all your teeth. Then spit out the pink saliva. Be careful not to get any on your clothes.

Now look at your teeth in the mirror. The pink dye from the tablet stains dental plaque. It doesn't stain clean enamel. If there are stains on your teeth, you have bacterial plaque on them. They should be cleaned by careful brushing. Compare the stains on your teeth with those of some of your friends or classmates.

41

THE MYSTERY OF THE STAINED TEETH

Have you heard the story of the stained teeth that led to a great dental discovery? It started in Colorado Springs, Colorado. Dentists there were puzzled because so many of their patients had strange brown stains on their teeth.

One dentist, Dr. Frederick McKay, was especially interested. He examined hundreds of people in Colorado Springs and neighboring towns. He found many people with the strange brown stains on their teeth. But in a few towns no one had teeth with this kind of stain.

He learned that the no-stain people drank water from lakes or rivers. All the people with stained teeth drank water from deep wells or springs. They had been drinking this water all their lives.

Dr. McKay was sure he had found a clue to the mystery. Something in the water that came from under the ground must be causing the stains. So he asked chemists to test water from each town. The chemists reported that the water from all the towns contained the same chemicals.

Twenty years went by. Dr. McKay was still puzzled and still interested in the mysterious stains. Other dentists were interested, too, because they had found that the people with *stained teeth had fewer cavities* than people without stains.

By this time Dr. McKay had examined the teeth of thousands of people in Colorado and other states. In Bauxite, Arkansas, a mining town, he found many stained-teeth people.

The mining company asked its chemist to examine the

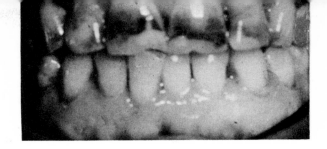

Fluoride-stained teeth

Bauxite drinking water. His tests showed something that other chemists had not found. In the water was a tiny amount of fluoride (FLOO-o-ride).

This chemical is found in the earth and rocks. It is also found in bones and teeth.

The company asked the chemist to repeat his tests on the Bauxite drinking water. Three times they asked him to test it. Each time he reported fluoride. The year was 1931.

More and more people became interested in fluoride.

The Public Health Service of the U.S. government made a study of 7,000 children in twenty-one cities. They found that where there was no fluoride in the drinking water of a city, the children had many cavities. If there was too much fluoride, there were not many cavities, but there were brown stains. If the water had about one part of fluoride to a million parts of water, there were *no stains* and *few cavities.*

Two neighboring cities in New York State agreed to try an experiment. This experiment started in May, 1945. Newburgh would add a tiny bit of fluoride to its water. Kingston would not.

At the end of ten years all the children in both cities were examined.

On the next page is a graph of what they found in Kingston. On the page after that is a project which will show you what happened in Newburgh.

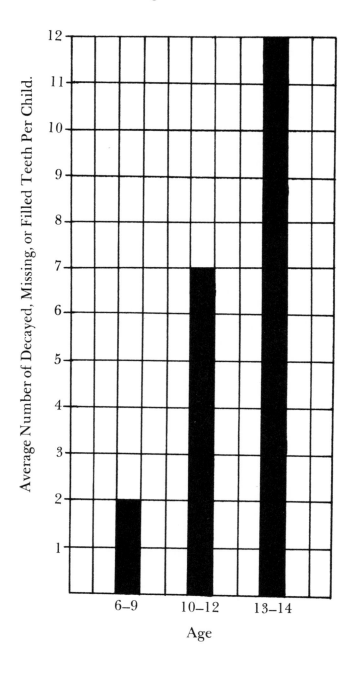

CAVITIES IN CHILDREN
NO FLUORIDATION IN WATER
Kingston, New York

PROJECT

PROJECT — TO MAKE A GRAPH SHOWING THE NUMBER OF CAVITIES IN CHILDREN'S TEETH IN TWO CITIES, WITH AND WITHOUT FLUORIDATED WATER

WHAT YOU NEED

Sheet of paper
ruler
red and black pencils

WHAT YOU DO

Copy or trace the graph on page 44 with the ruler and black pencil.

Then draw in lines for Newburgh with the red pencil right next to each Kingston line.

Use the table of figures at the bottom of this page to find out how long each line should be.

When you have finished, each age has two lines, a red line next to a black one.

CONCLUSIONS

What do the red lines show?

DATA FOR GRAPH

AGE	AVERAGE NUMBER OF DECAYED, MISSING, OR FILLED TEETH PER CHILD
6– 9	1
10–12	3
13–14	6

EIGHTY-EIGHT MILLION PEOPLE AND FLUORIDES

In a few years city after city decided to put tiny amounts of fluoride in its water. Here are the number of people using water with added fluoride. About one drop of fluoride is put in water for every million drops of water.

1952	13,000,000 people
1956	30,000,000 people
1967	62,000,000 people
1969	78,000,000 people (about 60 percent of the people who use public water)
Add to this	10,000,000 people who live in communities where the water naturally contains fluorides

Small amounts of fluorine also are found in many substances such as seafoods and tea.

The cost of adding fluoride to city water is about 10 to 15 cents per person for a whole year. As a result, all children have fewer cavities.

Here is picture graph of the results of fluoridation of water in another city.

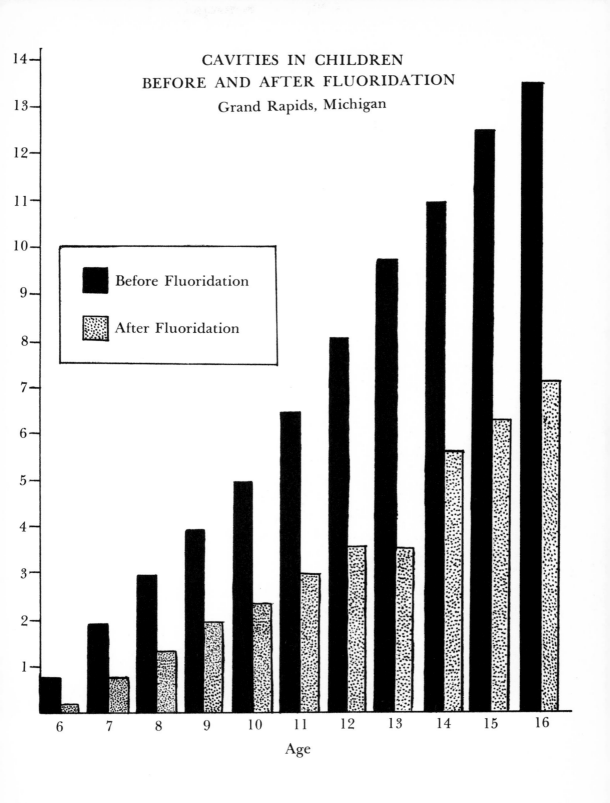

CAVITIES IN CHILDREN
BEFORE AND AFTER FLUORIDATION
Grand Rapids, Michigan

Before Fluoridation

After Fluoridation

Age

OTHER WAYS OF USING FLUORIDES

Do you live in a community where there is enough fluoride in the water? If not, there are other ways of using fluorides.

Fluorides may be

(1) painted on teeth by dentists;
(2) put in tooth pastes;
(3) taken in tablets or drops every day by children from the time of birth to the age of twenty years or older.

Fluorides in drinking water and fluorides taken internally (method 3) get into the tooth substance as it is being formed. The other two methods add the fluoride after the tooth has pushed through the gum and is fully grown except the root. You can see why methods 1 and 2 do not give as much protection against decay.

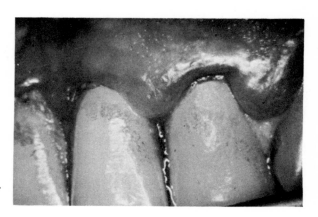

Periodontitis in a thirty-
five-year-old

ADULTS LOSE TEETH

Ask your parents if either of them has gums that are
tender and bleed easily. These are the first signs of a dental
disease common among adults. This disease is periodontitis (per-i-oh-don-TIE-tis), often called gum disease or
pyorrhea. It attacks the periodontal tissues around the
teeth. These tissues consist of the gum, periodontal ligament and bone.

Nine out of ten adults in the United States have some
periodontal disease. As a result one person in five loses all
his teeth by the time he is forty years old.

GUM DISEASE CAUSED BY GERMS

Periodontitis is a bacterial disease. These bacteria live in the bacterial plaque that collects in the sulcus (SUL-kus), the space between the gums and the teeth.

In healthy gums the sulcus is shallow, about one-sixteenth of an inch deep. When bacteria grow in the sulcus, it deepens and the gum becomes red and swollen. Tiny pieces of food may collect in it.

The toxins (poisons) from the bacteria slowly dissolve the periodontal ligament that holds the tooth. Later some of the bone around the root is destroyed. The tooth then becomes loose and useless.

Often periodontitis isn't noticed right away, because in the beginning there is little or no pain. Many adults go to their dentist for their regular examination and are surprised to learn that they have periodontal disease.

"I thought my teeth were OK because I didn't have any cavities," they say.

Measuring the sulcus

X ray of sulcus

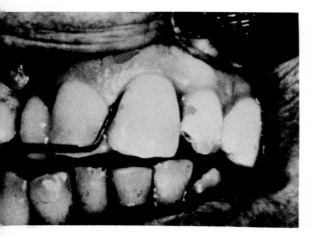
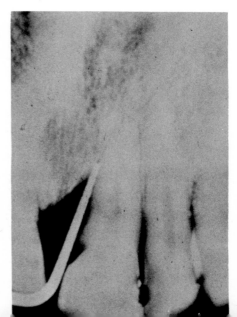

HOW TO PREVENT GUM DISEASE

Tell your parents that the best way to prevent periodontitis is to get rid of the conditions that help it develop. Crowded or missing teeth, poor occlusion, untreated caries, and poor diet may let the disease get a start. Even more important is bacterial plaque, which in adults often becomes hard and is called tartar.

Even with the best care, older people or even teen-agers may find their gums bleeding or a little sore. When this happens, it is time to see a dentist. Early treatment is the best way to prevent serious gum and bone disease.

The specialist in this disease is called a periodontist (per-i-o-DON-tist). It is his job to save teeth that without treatment might be lost.

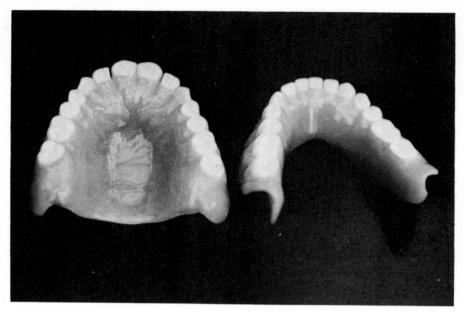

Plastic dentures

DENTURES — ARTIFICIAL TEETH

Teeth that are too badly damaged by caries or gum disease have to be removed. They are replaced by artificial ones.

Artificial teeth which are fastened together are called dentures. They may be full dentures to replace all the teeth. Partial dentures take the place of several lost teeth.

When only two or three teeth are lost, dentists often replace them with a bridge. This fills, or bridges, the gap and is fastened to the natural teeth on either side.

The first step in making a denture is to get an impression of the patient's mouth. (See page 28.) The dental technician uses this impression to make the denture so that it will fit the patient.

FIRST AID FOR TOOTH ACCIDENTS

Many young people lose teeth as the result of accidents. If you should accidentally knock a tooth out, do you know what to do? Often a tooth which is knocked out can be made usable again if the right things are done soon enough.

Of course if the nerve which goes into the jaw is torn apart it won't grow together, but the periodontal bone and ligament will often grow again.

Here is what you should do. Wrap the tooth in a wet cloth. Take it to your dentist immediately, within fifteen minutes if possible. Hurry! Speed is important.

The dentist will put a filling into the root canal to prevent infection. Then he will wire the tooth into its socket. The tissues gradually grow around the tooth and support it. You may be able to use it for many years.

TRANSPLANTS

We all have heard of heart transplants and kidney transplants, but did you know that teeth can be transplanted?

A transplanted tooth may fill a space where a permanent tooth has been lost. One of the most valuable transplants is the replacement of a six-year molar.

You know that the six-year molars are the first permanent teeth to appear in the mouth. Dentists say they are the key to good occlusion. Many children lose six-year molars because of decay. When this happens, the other teeth move out of their correct positions and lean toward the gap.

Usually the tooth to be transplanted is a wisdom tooth. It must be only partially formed and not yet visible outside the gum. It must be used in the same mouth from which it is taken.

Hundreds of transplants have been made. The roots of these teeth continued to grow, the periodontal ligament became attached, and the teeth stayed alive and usable for many years.

OLD-TIME DENTISTRY

For thousands of years people have been trying to cure toothache and replace lost teeth.

A common old-time cure for toothache was to pull out the tooth. Barber-surgeons pulled teeth, cut hair, and performed operations. The signs outside their offices were barber poles very like the ones we see today. The white stripes stood for bandages, the red stripes for blood. When there weren't any barbers around, the blacksmiths pulled teeth.

Other tradesmen, the silversmiths and jewelers, made artificial teeth of bone, ivory, or even hard wood. They fastened them together with gold or silver bands.

Artificial teeth have been found in the mouths of Egyptian mummies 3,000 years old. Hand-carved teeth or animal teeth wired to fit into human mouths were fairly common in Greece and Rome before the time of Christ.

Arab craftsmen began filling cavities with hard wax or gold foil. An Arabian book written in the year 857 advises treatment of tooth decay by scratching and cleaning the cavity with a chisel, knife, or file and then filling it with gold leaf.

A French dentist, Pierre Fauchard, is known as the founder of the dental profession. He published a book on dentistry in 1728. The first dentist in America was probably Robert Woofendale, who came to this country from England in 1766.

Nobody knew how to make an accurate cast of the jaws, so dentures fitted badly. They were painful to wear.

Dental office in 1885

George Washington was a denture wearer. He lost all his teeth when he was still a young man. Although he had several sets of dentures, none of them fitted well or was comfortable. He had to keep his lips pressed against his teeth to hold his dentures in place. This makes his face look stiff and stern in his pictures.

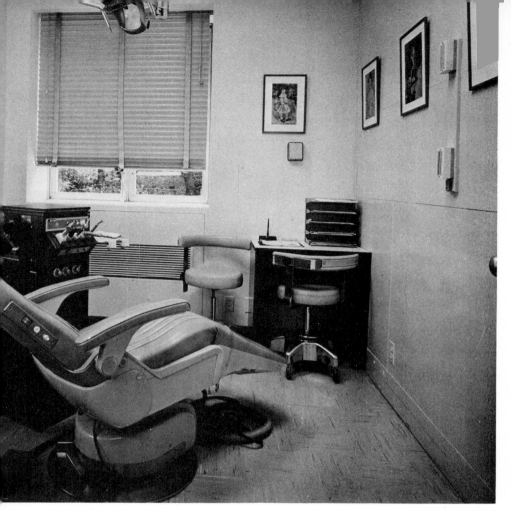

Modern dental office

MODERN DENTISTRY

Modern dentures are far more comfortable to wear than those of George Washington's time. In fact, dental scientists have improved all mouth and tooth care.

Broken teeth or cavities are repaired. Cavities in front

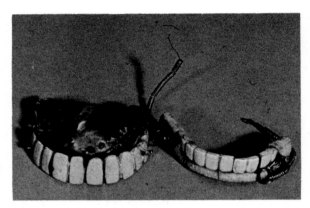

Set of ivory dentures made for George Washington

teeth are usually filled with silicate (SIL-i-kate) cement. This is made by mixing a porcelain-type powder with a weak acid solution (phosphoric). Most other fillings are made with a mixture of metals: silver, tin, and mercury. This mixture is soft when first made but hardens in a few hours.

Dental drills used to prepare cavities for filling run at very high speeds compared with old-time drills. The real old-timers were turned by foot power. About 1900 they were connected to electric motors. Some modern drills are run by compressed air and make 300,000 revolutions per minute. Drilling at this speed is more comfortable for the patient.

LOOK, MA, NO CAVITIES!

Here is the way dental scientists tell you to care for your teeth.

1. Eat a well-balanced diet, including plenty of fresh fruits and vegetables.
2. Eat sweets only with meals.
3. Choose between-meal snacks from foods such as those in the list on page 60.
4. Remove bacterial plaque from your teeth by brushing right after eating. If you can't brush, swish water around in your mouth.
5. Use fluoride in some form.
6. Have crowded teeth or poor occlusion corrected.

Many young people who follow these suggestions reach their teens with few or no cavities.

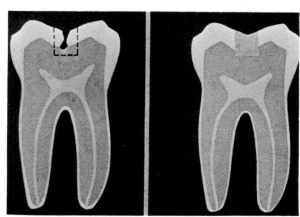

Filling a cavity

Left: Cavity and area to be removed

Right: The filling in place

FEWER CAVITY SNACKS
(Choose what is available locally)

GOOD AND JUICY
Apples
Berries
Oranges
Dill pickles
Grapefruit
Grapes
Peaches
Pears
Plums
Tomatoes

CRUNCHY
Carrots
Cauliflower
Celery
Apples
Cabbage wedges
Squash
Radishes
Bell peppers
Cucumber slices
Popcorn

THIRSTY?
Whole milk
Buttermilk
Tomato juice
Unsweetened fruit juice
Diet drinks

REALLY HUNGRY?
Meat cubes or slices
Cheese cubes or slices
Sardines
Nuts
Eggs

Index

Acknowledgments

I want to express my appreciation to all the people who helped me in the preparation of this book, to the dental and health scientists, to the educators and to those experts who read one or more chapters of the manuscript.

Thanks to Mrs. Betty Bacon, Supervisor of Children's Services, Public Library, Vallejo, California; to Mrs. Tessie Baldwin, Dental Hygienist, Richmond Unified School District, Richmond, California; to Dr. Chester Fong, Clinical Professor of Oral Biology and Dr. Donald R. Poulton, Associate Professor of Orthodontics of the School of Dentistry, University of California; to Dr. James L. Patton, Assistant Professor of Zoology, University of California, Berkeley; to Dr. Lloyd F. Richards, Director of Dallas City Dental Public Health Program, Dallas, Texas; To Dr. Zachary M. Stadt, Dental Health Officer, Public Health Department, Contra Costa County, Martinez, California; to Dr. R. L. Weiss, Chief of Public Education, Dental Health Center, HEW; and to the personnel of the School of Dentistry, University of California, and of the School of Dentistry, University of the Pacific, San Francisco.

I am particularly grateful to Dr. Gilbert Oliver, Lecturer in Periodontics at the School of Dentistry, University of California, whose help was invaluable.

WINIFRED G. HAMMOND
Berkeley, California

About the Author

WINIFRED HAMMOND was born in Covington, Indiana. She received a master's degree from the University of California and taught high school science and mathematics. Now, however, she devotes all her time to writing. She is the author of many popular books for the elementary grades, chiefly in the areas of science and social studies. Among her recent titles are *Cotton from Farm to Market, Wheat from Farm to Market,* and *Sugar from Farm to Market; The Riddle of Seeds,* and *Plants, Food and People.*

Winifred Hammond lives in Berkeley, California. She travels all over the United States, however, gathering material for her books.

For more information on dental caries experiments see the book *Nutrition Science and You,* by Olaf Mikelsen, produced by the National Teachers Association in cooperation with the U.S. Department of Agriculture, Agriculture Research Service. Published by Scholastic Book Services.